TIME

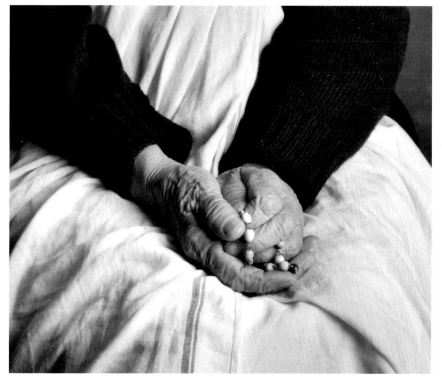

Mother Teresa
The Life and Works of a Modern Saint

TIME

MANAGING EDITOR Richard Stengel
DESIGN DIRECTOR D.W. Pine
DIRECTOR OF PHOTOGRAPHY Kira Pollack

Mother Teresa: The Life and Works of a Modern Saint

EDITOR Richard Lacayo
WRITER David Van Biema
DESIGNER D.W. Pine
PHOTO EDITOR Hillary Raskin
RESEARCHER Lisa McLaughlin
EDITORIAL PRODUCTION Rick Prue and Patricia N. Koh

TIME HOME ENTERTAINMENT
PUBLISHER Richard Fraiman
GENERAL MANAGER Steven Sandonato
EXECUTIVE DIRECTOR, MARKETING SERVICES Carol Pittard
DIRECTOR, RETAIL AND SPECIAL SALES Tom Mifsud
DIRECTOR, NEW PRODUCT DEVELOPMENT Peter Harper
DIRECTOR, BOOKAZINE DEVELOPMENT AND MARKETING Laura Adam
PUBLISHING DIRECTOR, BRAND MARKETING Joy Butts
ASSISTANT GENERAL COUNSEL Helen Wan
BOOK PRODUCTION MANAGER Suzanne Janso
DESIGN AND PREPRESS MANAGER Anne-Michelle Gallero
BRAND MANAGER Michela Wilde

ISBN 10: 1-60320-111-4
ISBN 13: 978-1-60320-111-7
Library of Congress Control Number: 2010927620

We welcome your comments and suggestions about TIME Books. Please write to us at:
TIME Books, Attention: Book Editors, P.O. Box 11016, Des Moines, IA 50336-1016

If you would like to order any of our hardcover Collector's Edition books, please call us at 1-800-327-6388,
Monday through Friday, 7 a.m. to 8 p.m., or Saturday, 7 a.m. to 6 p.m. Central Time

Contents

Unconditional Love

By Dr. Rick Warren

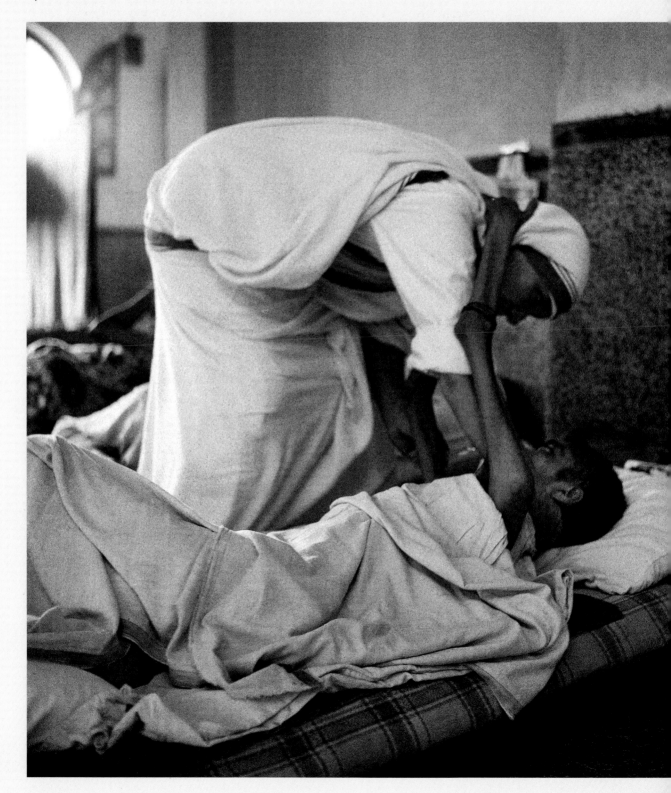

A HANDWRITTEN NOTE FROM MOTHER TERESA HANGS ON MY OFFICE WALL. IT SAYS, "BE HOLY because the God who created you is holy and he loves you." Mother Teresa didn't just believe those words; she incarnated them.

For over 50 years this tiny woman made an enormous impact by taking Jesus' commandment literally. She sacrificially gave her life to serve those in the streets of Calcutta whom everyone else pretended not to see: lepers, orphans, beggars, the sickest, the poorest, and those dying without dignity and love. What kept her going year after year? She always answered, "I see the face of Jesus in the poor, and I do it for Him."

It would be difficult to overestimate the significance of Mother Teresa's life and ministry. Living with the poorest of the poor, she also made an impact on the rich and powerful around the globe. She didn't have to make speeches. Her life was an indictment of our shallow materialism and the modern culture of death.

Today billions know of Mother Teresa's compassion. What is not so well known was her amazing leadership skills, evident in the multiplication of what she did in Calcutta to other parts of the planet. Her legacy is carried on by thousands of other members of her order who continue the same simple acts of charity and mercy today. My wife, Kay, was so deeply affected by her visit to Mother Teresa's Home for the Dying in Calcutta that our foundation is named Acts of Mercy.

Mother Teresa never told anyone, "I'll care for you if you become a Christian." Instead, she offered the same unconditional love our Savior did. By being the hands and feet of Jesus, this petite Albanian Catholic nun became one of the great evangelists of the 20th century.

Most people today do not know the difference between a hero and a celebrity. Celebrities are famous for being famous and typically use the spotlight to promote themselves. The difference between heroes and celebrities lies in the reason for their sacrifice. Celebrities often make sacrifices, but they are made for personal benefit—to win a game, an award, or an election. For instance, professional athletes, actors, and entertainers may be celebrities, but they are not really heroes. They sacrifice for what they do because they enjoy it, or for money or fame or personal satisfaction. Heroes, in contrast, sacrifice for the benefit of others. They are self-giving. Mother Teresa is exhibit A of a true hero—a saint.

By the time she wrote the note I have framed on my wall, leaders from around the world would listen to Mother Teresa. Why? I call it the Mother Teresa principle: The more you care about the powerless, the more power you have. The more you serve those with no influence, the more influence God gives you. The more you humble yourself, the more you're honored by others. This is the great lesson I hope you'll learn from this book.

Jesus said it this way, in Mark 8:35: "If you insist on saving your life, you will lose it. Only those who throw away their lives for my sake and for the sake of the Good News will ever know what it means to really live."

Don't just read this book. Let it change the direction of your life. Let it cause you to investigate the One who so transformed Mother Teresa that she was able to walk away from everything we spend our lives trying to attain. Discover her motivation, her method, but most of all, her Master.

On this 100th anniversary of her birth, I leave you with my favorite Mother Teresa quote: "God doesn't ask us to do great things. He asks us to do small things with great love." Find a place to do that today.

Rick Warren is the pastor of Saddleback Church in Orange County, Calif., and author of the international bestseller The Purpose Driven Life.

Her Life

1910
Agnes Bojaxhiu, the future Teresa, is born on Aug. 26 in Skopje, now the capital of Macedonia

1928
Leaves home to join the Sisters of Loreto, a religious order based in Ireland

1929–48
Teaches at the Loreto school in Calcutta, where she eventually becomes headmistress

1948
Receives permission from Pope Pius XII to pursue her ministry among the very poor

1950
Gains Vatican approval to start what will become the Missionaries of Charity

1957
Begins work with lepers

1965
Missionaries of Charity establishes its first mission house outside India, in Venezuela

1969
A book and television documentary by British journalist Malcolm Muggeridge brings Mother Teresa worldwide fame and media attention

1985
Establishes the first of what will be many AIDS ministries

1992
Meets and befriends Britain's Princess Diana

2002
The church recognizes the first miracle attributed to Teresa—the 1998 cure of a tumor suffered by Monica Besra (right)

2003
Over 250,000 people throng Saint Peter's Square in Rome for a Mass to celebrate Teresa's beatification, the last step before canonization

August 1946

Witnesses the brutality of Hindu-Muslim rioting in Calcutta (right), fighting that was a prelude to the division of India and Pakistan

September 1946

On a train trip, has vision of Christ urging her to form a ministry to aid and live among the poorest of the poor

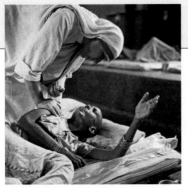

1952

Establishes Nirmal Hriday, her first Home for the Dying, in Calcutta

1955

Establishes her first home for orphans, also in Calcutta

1979

Awarded the Nobel Peace Prize

1980s

While continuing to open mission houses around the world, she comes under criticism for dealings with figures like Haiti dictator Baby Doc Duvalier

1983

When visiting Pope John Paul II, has her first heart attack

March 1997

In increasingly poor health, she steps down as head of the Missionaries of Charity

September 1997

Teresa dies. After a state funeral she is buried at the Mother House in Calcutta

1998

For Teresa the Vatican waives the five-year waiting period before it will begin to consider a candidate for sainthood

2007

Publication of *Mother Teresa: Come Be My Light*, a collection of Teresa's letters that reveals her decades-long anguish over the possibility that she had lost her profound connection to Christ

2010

U.S. Postal Service issues Mother Teresa stamp

Beginnings

CHAPTER ONE | In the photograph she is beautiful. In 1928, just before she left home to meet her destiny, Agnes Gonxha Bojaxhiu posed in front of a decorative textile. It looks like a formal portrait, taken in three-quarter profile. The image may owe something to the retoucher's art; full eyebrows evident in earlier photos and the prominent Bojaxhiu family nose are deemphasized. Instead the portrait shows off the 18-year-old's high cheekbones, a small, shapely mouth, and flawless skin, not yet weathered and marked by a hard life among the poor. But what truly defines the picture are her eyes. They are dark, lovely—and remarkably eloquent. Her gaze is serene yet determined, almost impatient. She is looking off to the photographer's

AGNES OF GOD *The future Teresa in 1928, the year she entered the Sisters of Loreto*

left, but also manifestly looking ahead. This is clearly *not* a snapshot of a provincial naif, a girl unaware that God is about to propel her into an utterly unanticipated life of holiness and service that breaks from everything she has ever known or imagined.

The girl in the photo—the future Mother Teresa—has some idea of what she is getting into.

This is a point worth making, given her origins. In the Gospel of John there is a famous putdown of Christ's hometown. Hearing where Jesus hails from, someone snorts, "Can anything good come out of Nazareth?" A similar issue haunts Mother Teresa's early history. As her fame grew, Teresa routinely identified herself as Albanian by origin. To many people this suggests the small, breathtakingly backward country that is now a free-market democracy, but which suffered under doctrinaire communism long after the rest of the Eastern bloc had escaped that dogma.

In fact, Albania did not exist as an independent nation when Agnes Bojaxhiu was born, and she grew up outside the territory it now occupies. Her home was in Skopje, then part of an outlying department of the Ottoman Empire and now the capital of Macedonia. In Skopje her family was part of the city's Roman Catholic Albanian minority. Situated near the border of Europe and Asia, as well as at one of the crossroads of Islam and Christianity, it was a picturesque place. Muslim minarets and ornate Christian Orthodox churches vied for the skyline over cobbled streets, and the Vardar River was spanned by a famous bridge. Yet it was also severely disadvantaged, poor and war-torn. In just the 18 years Agnes lived there, it was ruled successively by Ottoman Turks, Serbs, Bulgarians, and finally a multiethnic coalition, and the transitions were often bloody. By global standards it was, as Nazareth had been, a backwater.

Knowing that one of modern history's most beautiful and effective souls sprang incongruously from such thin soil lends weight to a particular notion of sainthood, one in which God reaches down and flicks a switch, totally transforming the pre-saint—who was until then pagan or nasty or merely average—into someone else entirely. But the truth is that despite her humble surroundings, Teresa's family was rich (relatively speaking), cultured, and active in civic affairs. Later hallmarks of her character, such as her managerial savvy, political sensitivity, and tolerance toward other faiths, as well as her extreme piety, reflected that upbringing. Her moderately privileged background permits a much less otherworldly view of saints. In this case, if God flicked a switch, he had laid the circuitry carefully beforehand.

Agnes Bojaxhiu was born Aug. 26, 1910, the third child in her family, after a sister named Aga and a brother, Lazar. Her father, Nikola, was part of a clan of merchants, while her mother Drana's family were landowners. Ines Murzaku, a professor at New Jersey's Seton Hall University who has written on Albanian Catholicism, describes them this way: "Her parents belonged to an elite, not very different from the bourgeoisie in Western Europe."

In Skopje, where the couple owned a spacious house and a garden with fruit trees, Nikola had family ties. The hospitality of his clan was so famous locally that it was a custom in Skopje to praise people by calling them "as generous as the Bojaxhius." Nikola was an extrovert who spoke five languages—Albanian, Serbo-Croatian, Turkish, Italian, and French—and whose wholesaling and contracting businesses took him as far as Cairo. In Skopje he turned his house into a kind of salon, where he would spin tales of his travels and pursue his favorite political cause, the creation of an Albanian state in the nearby region of Kosovo. In Skopje, whose territory would not be impacted if such a state were established, it was not a polarizing issue. However, there was friction between the Muslim majority and the mostly Eastern Orthodox Christian

MY LITTLE TOWN *Skopje as it appeared in 1930, two years after the young Teresa departed. Today it's the capital of Macedonia.*

minority, and it was in that connection that Nikola's generosity of spirit and tolerance for other faiths paid dividends. Despite the fact that Catholic Albanians were a tiny minority in Skopje, he managed to assume a seat on the city council. Jim Towey, a prominent Catholic layman who worked with Teresa in her later decades, notes, "Mother always understood both the potential and the limitations of politics and government. I have to believe it came from her upbringing."

Complementing her father's man-of-the-people savvy was her mother's almost severe piety. It was Drana who made sure her children attended Mass several times a week at the Church of the Sacred Heart, conveniently located just down the street. She enforced the family's daily joint recitation of the rosary. Just as her daughter would later, Drana considered any moment not somehow dedicated to Christ to be wasted. When she thought one of her husband's gatherings had become overly frivolous, she simply shut off the house's electricity. It was she who maintained the family's commitment to the poor, adopting several orphans and opening her table to the needy. When Lazar asked Drana why she did it, she replied, "Some of them are our relations, but all of them are our people." She regularly walked a local circuit distributing food and sometimes cash to the needy and giving special attention to an alcoholic named File, nursing the woman and cleaning her sores. Accompanying Drana on those charitable rounds —and apparently making mental notes—was the diminutive Agnes.

No one called her Agnes. She went by her middle name, Gonxha (pronounced gōn-KHÄ), which means "flower bud" in Albanian. In *Such a Vision of the Street—Mother Teresa: The Spirit and the Work*, Teresa's friend and biographer Eileen Egan quotes Lazar's description of his sister in early youth as "plump, round, and tidy," as well as "a little too serious for her age." Actually she seems to have nicely combined her mother's piety and her father's enterprise. She loved attending church and visiting the local Marian shrine of Cernagore. She helped Lazar steal jam from the cupboard at night—but warned him not to eat any after midnight if they were taking Communion

SISTER TERESA
It was on joining the Sisters of Loreto that Agnes took her new name, in honor of Saint Thérèse of Lisieux.

at Mass the next morning. She soloed in the parish choir, played mandolin, and enjoyed writing, even placing articles in a local newspaper. A cousin remembered her as sociable, dependable, and a leader who tutored some of her classmates. Although her brother recalled her as becoming "very good-looking," it gradually became clear that "wife" would not be her calling. She would become a missionary nun.

That intent crystallized just as one important influence exited her life and another entered. In 1919, when Gonxha was 9, her father died mysteriously after attending an Albanian patriotic conference in Belgrade. (Some believed he was poisoned.) His business partner attached his assets. To support the family, Drana had to resort to selling handmade embroidery. For several years, until she could parlay that into a successful carpet business, the family who had always helped the poor experienced something very like poverty themselves.

Meanwhile a new pastor had arrived in the parish. Father Franjo Jambrekovic was a Jesuit who preached that order's theology of godly action in everyday life: "What have I done for Jesus? What am I doing for Jesus? What will I do for Jesus?" He introduced the parish girls to the Sodality of the Blessed Virgin Mary, one of whose aims was to involve young women in practical service to Christ through charity to the poor. Jambrekovic also enthusiastically recounted to them the efforts of Jesuit missionaries, especially a group of Croatians sent recently to Bengal, in India. Occasionally one of the missionary fathers would even stop in Skopje to describe his latest spiritual exploits in the Sundarbans, an exotic landscape of shifting sandbars where the river Ganges meets the Bay of Bengal, a place beloved of Rudyard Kipling and later of Salman Rushdie.

For the future Mother Teresa, here was a vocation that might give her the opportunity to combine her mother's piety and father's wanderlust. According to her biographer Egan, by age 17, Gonxha was already urging a cousin who was giving free music lessons to "take [some money] and give it to me for the missions in India." By 18, after going on several long, thoughtful retreats at Cernagore, she had decided on a more personal investment. "I wanted to become a missionary," she wrote later. "I wanted to go out and give the life of Christ to the people." When she first expressed that intention to Drana, her mother forbade it, then took to her room for 24 hours before emerging to give her consent. The Jesuits (who are men) put Gonxha in touch with the Sisters of the Institute of the Blessed Virgin Mary—the Loreto Sisters for short—who were active in Bengal and who accepted her. In October 1928 a weeping Drana, accompanied by Gonxha's older sister, Aga, saw their "flower bud" onto a train leaving Macedonia.

By that point she was, in truth, a bud no more, but had bloomed into a young person of unlimited idealism and formidable confidence. The 1928 photograph that opened this chapter dates almost precisely from her time of departure. So does her reply to a letter from the bewildered Lazar, who had just joined the army of the newly formed (and short-lived) monarchy of Albania. Did his sister know what she was doing? She responded, "You think you are important because you are an officer serving a king with 2 million subjects. But I am serving the king of the whole world." At some point in the seven-week sea journey that took her through the Suez Canal, the Red Sea, and the Indian Ocean, the intrepid voyager wrote this verse:

Goodbye, O mother dear.
May God be with you all.
A Higher Power compels me
Toward torrid India.

Her Family

Though Mother Teresa came from a close-knit family, their time together was brief. She was just 8 when her father died, in 1919. Some years later her brother joined the army of the short-lived kingdom of Albania, then emigrated to Italy. And after she left for India in 1928, she never saw her mother or sister again.

Her mother, Dranafile

Her father, Nikola

Agnes, the future Teresa (left), age 10

At 13, with older sister Aga (right)

Teresa, 14 (seated), with Aga and brother Lazar

MINISTERING ANGEL
Mother Teresa (right) visits malnourished patients in 1976 at Nirmal Hriday, her home for the destitute and dying in Calcutta.

mountains of laundry (by hand), all with a smile, as the woman they called "Mother" had encouraged them to do.

On that morning a sister grabbed me by the arm, steered me into a dark room, and asked me to baptize an elderly man about to die. I protested that I wasn't yet a priest. What's more, the sister was surely holier than I was. "No," she said firmly, "you must do it. He knows you." At that moment, I knew I would do it. And I sensed what lay behind the example of these humble, hard-working, iron-willed sisters: the astonishing spirituality of their remarkable founder.

"JESUS WAS MY FIRST LOVE," WROTE AGNES GONXHA BOJAXHIU.

She first knew she had a "vocation for the poor" at age 12. Six years later she felt called to join the Sisters of Loreto, an Irish-based religious order, in Calcutta. And for the next 17 years her spirituality was not unlike that of thousands of other Catholic sisters. For the vast majority of sisters, brothers, and priests, a "call" manifests itself as a simple heartfelt desire, much as someone else might be attracted to the life of a physician or lawyer. Yet a call to become a Catholic sister does imply a somewhat higher level of commitment. When she joined the Loreto Sisters, for instance, Gonxha took a new name, Teresa, as a sign of her entrance into a new life. She chose it out of admiration for Saint Thérèse of Lisieux, the 19th-century Carmelite nun who pioneered the "little way," which stressed doing small things, with great love, for God.

Like every other Catholic sister, Teresa made vows of poverty, chastity, and obedience and agreed to live within a religious community. Like the "call," such vows can also be overdramatized. But at their heart they are meant to be liberating rather than restrictive. Poverty means, among other things, freedom from worrying about possessions, since everything is owned in common. Chastity means the freedom to love many people with abandon rather than one person exclusively. Obedience means freedom from excessive self-interest. All are designed to streamline a person's life for greater service to God. They are also intended to help a person imitate Jesus, who himself chose to be poor, chaste, and obedient to his Father.

For nearly two decades Teresa (called "Sister" in her early years and later, by tradition, "Mother") lived out her call both contemplatively, by praying, and actively, by teaching Indian children at the Loreto School. In 1942, somewhat unusually, she made a fourth vow: to give God anything—"not to refuse Him anything … under pain of mortal sin." This desire for a deeper commitment suggests an intensity of spirit welling within her and the fervor of her love for Jesus.

Yet even then she probably could not imagine what the vow might mean.

IN THE SUMMER OF 1946, CALCUTTA WAS SHAKEN BY RELIGIOUS RIOTING. NORMALLY THE nuns would remain cloistered behind their walls, but Teresa, by then headmistress, ventured into the city to gather food for her charges. The brutality she witnessed shook her deeply. Seeing that she was nearing exhaustion, her religious superiors sent her in September to a retreat in Darjeeling. The train trip from the Bengali lowlands to the city in the Himalayan foothills is a dramatic one, filled with hairpin turns and sudden vistas as the clouds part to reveal the splendor of the mountains. The people who later became Teresa's followers always knew that something happened on that trip to change her path forever, but it was only after her death that the publication of her letters revealed to the world that, beginning on that train, she heard the voice of Jesus, and shortly afterward had several visions of Christ on the cross.

Here Mother Teresa's spiritual experiences depart decisively from the norm. She said she literally heard Christ's voice and conversed with him. Even the lives of the saints present relatively

FATEFUL TRACK *It was on a train like this one headed into Darjeeling that Teresa said she heard Christ's call.*

The Sisters

Until a branch for Catholic brothers was founded in 1963, the Missionaries of Charity were all women, and women with a very demanding day. Up at 4:40 a.m., the sisters attended daily Mass. Then some would fan out through the slums, finding and aiding the sick and destitute. Others pitched in at the orphanages, clinics, and hospices of their order. At left, Teresa at the Mother House. At right, a wash day there in 1958.

few cases of an auditory "locution," and when they do, Jesus often speaks succinctly. Teresa's letters to her superiors and spiritual directors, however, present her experience as more like a lengthy and impassioned dramatic dialogue. Christ affectionately calls her "my little one," and she answers him as "my own Jesus." He tells her he wants her to leave Loreto and found a new, radically different religious order. As most of us would, she doubts her ability to fulfill so difficult an assignment. Christ both prods her ("Is your generosity gone cold?") and offers his support ("Remember I am with you"). At some point she also experienced three visions of the crucifixion, one in which Jesus' mother, Mary, supports Teresa while her son asks, "Will you refuse to do this for me?"—as if specifically invoking that fourth vow.

The Catholic Church rightly reserves judgment about private locutions and visions (after all, they are unprovable) but reveres those it finally deems authentic. Believers have puzzled for centuries over some of the more cryptic communications to the saints, but in Mother Teresa's case, Jesus was crystal clear: He wanted her to leave the convent. "Carry Me into the holes of the poor," she reported hearing. "I want Indian nuns, Missionaries of Charity, who would be my fire of love among the poor, the sick, the dying, and the little children."

Naturally Teresa worried about leaving Loreto and engaging in work beyond what most sisters were doing at the time. But Jesus was adamant. "There are plenty of nuns to look after the rich and well-to-do people," she would report him replying, "but for my very poor, there are absolutely none. For them I long—them I love. Wilt thou refuse?"

Not every believer—not even every devout Catholic—subscribes to phenomena like locutions. But most Western faithful agree that there are moments when God communicates with an individual in a language that he or she can understand. With someone else, God might have employed emotions, feelings, memories, desires, or insights. With Mother Teresa, apparently, something of this magnitude was needed to persuade her to change her life utterly.

And it did. Since then, every year on Sept. 10 the Missionaries of Charity have commemorated her experience on that train as Inspiration Day. When she returned from Darjeeling, she began petitioning the Calcutta archdiocese for permission to form her own order. These new sisters, she explained, would live among, dress like, and serve the poorest of the poor.

In explaining her new ministry, Teresa often employed Jesus' words in the New Testament. From his command to care for the "least of these" in the Gospel of Matthew—"I was hungry and you gave me something to eat, I was thirsty ..."—she derived a simple mandate to help. "He has told us that he is the hungry one. He is the naked one. He is the thirsty one. Each one is Jesus in his distressing disguise."

In the particular phrase "I thirst," which Jesus uttered in agony during his last hours on the cross, Mother Teresa discovered a mystical touchstone that she invested with multiple spiritual meanings. First, the fact that Jesus literally thirsted demonstrated that God had indeed become human, out of compassion for humankind. Second, Jesus' command in the Gospels imposes a duty to alleviate the thirst (and hunger and illness) of his beloved poor. Third, Teresa understood Christ as "thirsting" for the love of humans and their souls. (This included those of non-Christians, but she was adamant that they were to be won over by good example, not by some kind of food-for-salvation tradeoff.) And finally, as she explained to church authorities, since Mother herself thirsted for Jesus in her life, she must give herself over entirely to what he had called her to do.

Her superiors were not immediately convinced. They worried about her preparedness, her safety, and the fact that she had already promised to remain with the Loreto order for life.

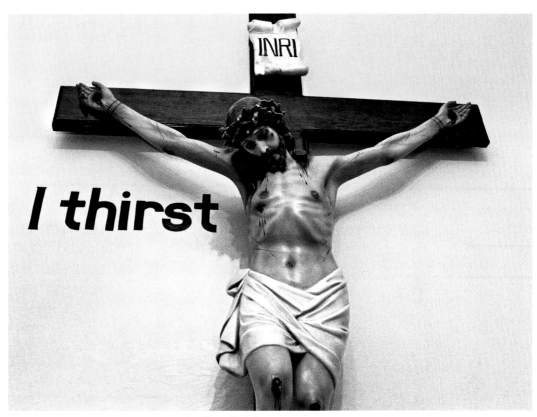

WORDS TO LIVE BY *A cross in the chapel of the Missionaries of Charity mission house in Washington, D.C.*

Finally, after 15 months of explanation, planning, and incessant lobbying (it was the hierarchy's first taste of Teresa's formidable will), she received approval from Pope Pius XII in April 1948. The Missionaries of Charity had begun.

FORTY-ONE YEARS LATER I STOOD OVER THE DYING MAN IN THE MISSIONARIES OF CHARITY hospice in Kingston. Its chapel had just one decoration: a crucifix, beside which was the single phrase "I thirst." I used a tablespoon to pour water over his head and baptize him. But what would his baptismal name be? "Joseph," I suggested to the sari-clad nun next to me. "Yes," she replied, as if she expected this answer, "because Saint Joseph listened." Christ's earthly father had been asked to accept the mysterious pregnancy of his betrothed, Mary. He was understandably bewildered. Yet God explained it all to him in a dream, and he listened.

The dying man before us had, like Joseph, listened to God's call. So had the small holy woman whom neither of us had ever met but who had drawn us together. She had heard God's voice; she had been initially confused and doubtful; but she had accepted the invitation and led a life of utter fidelity. And through that grace humanity has been infinitely enriched.

James Martin, SJ, is a Jesuit priest, culture editor of America *magazine, and the author of several books, including* My Life With the Saints *and* The Jesuit Guide to (Almost) Everything.

Carnage

A body lies in the street after days of fierce rioting in Calcutta in August 1946. All that year, as Britain prepared to grant India independence, tensions had risen between Hindus and Muslims who wanted their own nation. Searching for food for the pupils and nuns huddled at the Loreto school, Teresa ventured into the bloody aftermath of the riots, an experience that affected her deeply.

Gandhi

The great pacifist leader Mohandas
Gandhi (at center, above) was the preemi-
nent figure in the Indian drive for independence. Much to his dismay, divisions
between Hindus and Muslims would lead
to the partition of India and Pakistan
in 1947. Then on Jan. 30, 1948, he was
assassinated by a Hindu nationalist. That
same year Teresa would start her ministry. Though a Catholic, she liked to quote
the Hindu "Gandhiji" on her calling:
"He who serves the poor serves God."
At right, Gandhi's funeral procession.

Her Ministry Is Born

CHAPTER THREE

It was not your typical first day on the job. On Dec. 21, 1948, the 38-year-old Teresa—having departed the Loreto convent and now lodged temporarily in another part of Calcutta with the Little Sisters of the Poor—stepped out into an infinitely harsher reality. After almost 20 years in India, she was now embarked on a new life as head of her own ministry, the Missionaries of Charity. As she recalled at the time in a journal, almost immediately she encountered her first client: "an old man lying on the street—not wanted —all alone, just sick and dying." She gave him some water and a medication that fought amoebas. "The old man," she wrote, "was so strangely grateful."

COME IN *Teresa in 1958 at her home for children in Calcutta*

SHADOW OF DEATH
A painfully under-
nourished man lies
in a bathing room at
Teresa's Home for the
Dying in Calcutta.

Moving on to a nearby market, she found a woman in the advanced stages of starvation. The diminutive Teresa, dressed not in a habit but in a humble sari whose only distinguishing characteristics were three blue stripes and a crucifix clasp, later recalled wanting to provide the poor soul with "a cup of milk or something like that." But she had none. She noted forlornly, "I must try to be somewhere where I can easily get at [such] things."

It is one thing to hear God's demand to live and minister among the poor, but another to fulfill it. In 1947, Teresa formalized a "rule" for what she then called the "Sisters of Charity," one that she had scribbled earlier in a yellow notebook. The rule was her promise to Him to "unremittingly ... [seek] out, in towns and villages, even amid squalid surroundings, the poorer, the abandoned, the sick, the infirm, the dying" and care for them "assiduously." But no rule could inoculate her against the culture shock she experienced among the desperately poor. For the first 18 years of her life she had lived in the bosom of her loving Macedonian family; for the next 20 she had enjoyed the tight-knit, enclosed Loreto community. Suddenly she was radically alone among teeming, suffering millions. Her fond memories of her old order struck her as almost satanic: "The comfort of Loreto came to tempt me," she wrote. "My God ... give me courage."

To understand her near panic, it helps to know something about the swirling chaos she had just entered. In the summer of 1947, India had achieved independence from British rule after a largely peaceful campaign led by Mohandas Gandhi. But at birth the new nation broke into two parts: India, with a Hindu majority, and largely Muslim Pakistan. Fighting between Hindus and Muslims would claim a million lives and produce some 14 million refugees, one of history's greatest and most wrenching migrations. In January 1948, just months before Teresa embarked on her personal ministry, Gandhi was assassinated by a Hindu radical.

Calcutta had long attracted the poor from the countryside. But as Hindu refugees streamed in from the new Pakistan, the once proud city became, as one writer put it, "hideously swollen." Calcutta had previously contained some 3,000 officially recognized *bustees*, or slums. Now it risked becoming one huge *bustee*. The homeless thronged its train station and its streets; the dying were unheeded; children choked to death in public on easily curable parasitic worms.

Without knowing it, Calcutta needed Mother Teresa. "The municipality was seeking a solution to the problem of destitutes dying in the streets," notes Kathryn Spink, author of *Mother Teresa: A Complete Authorized Biography*. If there was someone willing to take on the problem, he or she would provide a tremendous civic service, not to mention, as Spink observes, "salve the conscience of Calcutta's more socially minded citizens."

Few would have imagined that Teresa was that person. Several of her Loreto sisters later recalled that she had not seemed extraordinary to them and had also appeared physically delicate. A Croatian priest and friend would later admit, "We thought she was cracked." And yet after those first days she never turned back.

For Teresa, the good she achieved in Calcutta in her order's first decade, and throughout the world in subsequent years, was a simple matter. It was accomplished through a kind of direct action and not something that required a sophisticated charitable institution as its prerequisite. As she later told Ann and Jeanette Petrie, sisters who made a marvelous 1986 documentary about her called *Mother Teresa*: "I picked up a man from the street, and he was eaten up alive from worms. Nobody could stand being with him, and he was smelling so badly. I went to him to clean him. And he said, 'Why do you do this?' And I said, 'Because I love you.'" Throughout her career she also insisted, to the exasperation of her critics and even sometimes her friends,

IN FLIGHT *The partition of India created millions of refugees, like these Sikhs fleeing to a Hindu part of the Punjab in October 1947. Many landed in the Calcutta of Mother Teresa.*

that her goals did not require of her the gifts of an organizer. "We do not make plans," she said. "We do not prepare infrastructure." Divine providence, she explained, guided her and her sisters in their work and in finding the means to support it.

Eileen Egan, who was not only Teresa's most perceptive biographer but also a good friend, thought she detected in Teresa's attitude an element of self-protection. As Egan describes her, Teresa had promised Jesus "to do everything possible for the poorest and the weakest" in the midst of "an abyss of need." In the big picture the task was truly hopeless. But to see the needy as discrete individuals whose problems had solutions dictated by God reduced this grim complexity to something much simpler—a matter, as Egan put it, "of gathering children around her under a plum tree, or of lifting a dying human creature from the gutter."

Ultimately, whether you accepted Teresa's analysis of her own role in her ministry depends once more on whether you like your miracles straight up (making Teresa a kind of holy innocent) or performed through the involvement of a sizable human intellect and will. As Egan writes, with a kind of fond bemusement, "I marveled at the formidable gift of communication and community organization of Mother Teresa, a gift of which its possessor was completely unaware."

But Teresa herself insisted to the end that she was merely "a little pencil" in God's hand, referring decisions to him case by case. Or as she liked to put it in Hindi: *Ek. Ek. Ek.* One. One. One.

Ek. On that first day of her ministry Teresa's wanderings took her back to a slum called Moti Jihl, or Pearl Lake, for the stagnant pond it surrounded. It was a *bustee* with a minority Christian population, situated beneath a railroad bridge just outside the gates of the Loreto Sisters' compound. From there she must often have looked over at it in consternation. At Moti Jihl she gathered a group of children around her, picked up a stick, and began drawing the characters of the Bengali alphabet in the mud. The first day there were 21 children; the next morning 40 were waiting at the bridge. Gradually Teresa added simple math and the Catholic catechism to their ABCs. As the days went by she brought along bars of soap, which she awarded to her students as prizes. Later, with the deftness of a trained community organizer, she persuaded the city of Calcutta to provide a pump to go with the soap. Later still, when the school reached 100 pupils, the government was legally obligated to provide it with a building. Which was followed by classes—and buildings—in other slums.

Ek. Teresa was not alone long. Three months into her project she was joined by Subashini Das, a former student at the school run by the Loreto Sisters, and within weeks by another student named Magdalena Gomes. As the number of pupils climbed, the Indian archdiocese put a roof over their heads, first renting part of a privately owned home and then purchasing two houses and a central courtyard at 54a Lower Circular Road, the building that is still the Mother House for the Missionaries of Charity.

Teresa required severe privations from the sisters of her new order. They were to brush their teeth with ashes. Their saris, undecorated except for one wide and two narrow blue stripes, were often made of repurposed grain sacks. Only the intervention of a medically trained nun persuaded "Mother" to provide a more sustaining diet than rice and water. Even so, when there were no funds for fuel, the new sisters sometimes ate raw bulgur wheat soaked overnight. "We couldn't wait for money," Teresa explained. "Life and poverty were everywhere."

She also transmitted to her followers her own mother's fear of wasted time. Up from 4:40 a.m. to 10:00 p.m., they prayed as they walked, and they walked fast—fast enough to become known as the "running sisters." In addition to "loving trust" and "total surrender," Teresa demanded cheerfulness. She half-jokingly told her novices, "Anybody who doesn't smile, make them smile." And for Mother and Jesus they enthusiastically complied.

Ek. Very early on in her ministry, writes Egan, Mother Teresa "picked up a woman who had been half-eaten by rats and ants and took her to the nearest hospital," only to be turned away because the hospital was overcrowded and the woman penniless and beyond saving. Teresa promptly applied to the Calcutta municipal authorities to build a hospice. Nothing happened until 1952, when a similar case caught the attention of the press. Suddenly the city found room for Teresa's proposed hospice in spacious quarters next to the Temple of Kali, the Hindu deity after whom the city was named.

The new hospice—her Home for the Dying—raised the kind of faith issues that had nearly destroyed India. Hinduism divided society into castes, something like social classes, only much

Teresa in 1958 at Nirmala Shishu Bhavan, her home for children in Calcutta, which admitted any child who arrived there.

more rigidly defined, and allowed only members of the lowest castes to deal with the dead, who were considered spiritually unclean. The mere thought of Teresa's sisters, some of them highborn, tending the mortally ill in a facility right next to a sacred shrine infuriated some radical Hindus, who also accused Teresa of requiring deathbed conversions from her patients. As the story goes, an enraged mob entered the hospice and threatened to kill her. But when she replied calmly, "If you kill us, we would only hope to reach God sooner," they retreated. The tolerance learned from her father eventually defused the situation for good, as skeptics observed her dignified treatment of all Kalighat residents, and the way the dead were dealt with according to their beliefs, whether they were sent to the cremation *ghats* of the Hindus or to Muslim or Christian cemeteries.

Ek. From her first days of teaching as a Loreto sister, Teresa had been aware that there were some children—orphans and the homeless—for whom education would be useless unless they first found shelter. In her own ministry she had also begun to take in pregnant homeless women and encourage them to give birth, resulting in a baby boom. Thus she established her first home for children, soon filled past capacity. But by now Teresa had also developed her first powerful political champion. B.C. Roy was a physician turned chief minister of the new state of West Bengal, where Calcutta is located. It was Roy who truly opened the city's coffers to the little nun. When she inaugurated her first large-scale orphanage, called Shishu Bhavan, he even gently chastised her, writing, "Bigger, Mother. Try to buy the adjoining property. I shall help you." Police, social workers, doctors, and hospitals eventually all sent children to Shishu Bhavan, and by 1975 there were branches in 61 Indian cities.

Ek. In 1957 five new supplicants at the house at Lower Circular Road touched off another expansion of Teresa's efforts. They were lepers who had lost their jobs because of their condition. Here was a taboo that reached beyond Hinduism—both the Hebrew Bible and medieval Christianity regarded leprosy as a manifestation of spiritual impurity. Yet the sisters embraced lepers as readily as any other humans created in God's image. As it happened, Teresa's involvement with lepers coincided with the appearance of new drugs called sulfones that could both treat the disfiguring illness and render it noninfectious. She became a sulfone crusader, equipping automobiles as mobile treatment units in hope of helping lepers before their families tossed them out. She addressed her newest clients with the same hearty cheer she applied to indigents and later royalty, casually chatting with leprous beggars about their day's take.

Ek. Ek. Ek. The Mother Teresa who led the leprosy campaign was, from the outside at least, light-years removed from the solitary nun, with no resources and no real home, who had ventured forth a decade before. When she began a fund drive whose motto was "Touch a leper with your compassion," Calcutta's fashionable charitable set got involved, and thousands of rupees came in. At a celebration in 1959 for the opening of India's first "static all-weather dispensary" for leprosy drugs, the archbishop of Calcutta presided, and the audience comprised a novel mix of the city's lepers and its social elite. By now there were nearly 100 sisters, and the number of lay helpers responding to Teresa's invitation to "do something beautiful for Christ" was growing weekly.

Nearly 40 years of ministry lay ahead of her. But in that first decade Teresa had created something radically new. For centuries both church and government had "worked with the poor." But led by Christ, Teresa redefined the phrase word by word. By substituting "the poorest of the poor" she established a social category that carried with it a new, urgent moral imperative. By taking the word "with" literally, she removed the traditional arm's-length distance between benefactor and beneficiary, creating instead a mutual bond. Thus, her "work with the poor" was like no one else's. All that remained was for the world to notice.

Calcutta

In the late 1940s and '50s it was a city under
tremendous stress. As many as half of its
roughly 4 million inhabitants were destitute.
Despite extensive relief efforts, its thousands
of slums were filled with the homeless, its
jails bursting, and its hospitals over-full. In
such a place the newly created Missionaries
of Charity were a small symbol of hope.
Above, a family seeking to flee fighting
between Hindus and Muslims in 1946 waits
at Calcutta's railway station. At left, the
teeming streets of the city in 1953.

Mother to the World

The saintly attract miracle stories. In the first years of Mother Teresa's ministry, people who knew of her work often told the tale of a mad bull that had been terrorizing a neighborhood in a Calcutta slum. Eventually it burst into an alley where Teresa was helping the poor. When Teresa saw the enraged animal, the story goes, she simply raised her hand. The bull, suddenly docile as a lamb, allowed itself to be led away.

Years later, when the humble sister from Calcutta had become a celebrated international figure, miracle stories about Teresa were still being told. But by then, just like her reputation, the scale of the reported miracles had grown and their locales had gone global.

GUIDING LIGHT
In Tijuana, Mexico, in 1985 a sister takes her small charge in hand.

FAR CORNERS
Laundry day at a Missionaries of Charity home in Mongolia for orphaned and abandoned girls

One of the stories is from 1982, when Teresa was visiting Beirut in the midst of the Lebanese civil war. Hearing that several dozen mentally ill children were trapped in a partially ruined hospital on the city's Muslim side, she decided to rescue them—even though the district was still being shelled by the Israeli army. In their documentary about Teresa, the filmmaking Petrie sisters capture a scene in which aid experts and clerics hint to her that such an act would be suicidal. Teresa replies serenely that she has been praying to Mother Mary "that there will be a cease-fire tomorrow." Her advisers are skeptical.

As the film goes on to show, a partial cease-fire occurs—providentially?—the next day. Teresa heads quickly for the hospital. There she approaches a terrified boy in the throes of spasms, holds his head, and looks into his eyes until, as with that bull, his frenzy subsides. Later still we see the multifaith caravan she has organized spiriting the children back to the safety of Lebanon's Christian zone. A doctor involved in the rescue mission later described Teresa as "a cross between a military commander and Saint Francis."

This scene is notable on at least two counts. One is that, unlike most miraculous episodes, this one is documented on camera. The other is that it took place far outside India, Teresa's original homebase. That was possible because in 1965 the Vatican had declared the Missionaries of Charity a "society of pontifical right," thus making it answerable only to the Vatican rather than to any local archdiocese, and freeing it to operate worldwide. With that, Mother Teresa became an international phenomenon.

Most corporate executives will tell you that international growth is tough. Before they go global, they plan intensively, carefully define their market, and sweat over the cultural issues that will undoubtedly bedevil their foreign workforce. Typically enough, Mother Teresa did none of that. All the same, she presided over one of the most spectacularly successful global rollouts in modern religious history. At a time when other Catholic women's orders were beginning to see a disastrous decline in personnel, she not only attracted hundreds more sisters (and brothers, who by then had a small order of their own) but also sent them out to dozens of new countries and hundreds of new projects. Suddenly part of the pledge she had made to God in 1949—to show compassion and love to the poorest of the poor "all over the world"—seemed less a grandiose pipe dream than a simple statement of fact.

The Missionaries' first non-Indian venture was in Venezuela, where the sisters' "*Ek. Ek. Ek.*" flexibility became a quick asset. Employed in the countryside, not in the capital of Caracas, they faced rural isolation rather than urban overpopulation. They set up classes in sewing, typing, and English, and sped from village to village in a Jeep, their gasoline paid for by the local governor. In a recent interview Sister Dorothy, who was the fourth sister to join Teresa in India and later worked for her all over the world, remembered the mission there as a sort of exercise in ad hoc miracles. "We didn't plan," she says. "Our work was like emergency work on a continuous basis." As challenges arose, the sisters simply expanded their responsibilities to meet them. When a near hurricane hit their area, they worked as roofers. When several parishes were threatened by a shortage of priests, they obtained permission to administer communion themselves.

Teresa's Missionaries set up next in a less predictable locale: Rome. Some Vatican eyebrows were raised, since 22,000 nuns already lived in the city and the church ran two large charitable services there. But the Missionaries soon found an underserved niche of poverty in a longtime squatters' settlement. There they provided day care, sewing lessons, and after-school classes for children and made visits to shut-ins, engaging in the fine-grain charity that larger groups

IN HAITI *Sisters throw soil on the graves of Archbishop Joseph Serge Miot and Vicar General Charles Benoit, victims of the 2010 earthquake.*

AIDS WORKER *Sister Maria Gloria works at the Mother Teresa Hospital in Khayaelitsha Township, Cape Town, South Africa.*

didn't handle. Led by a Malaysian sister who spoke perfect Italian, they planted pink climbing roses on the wall of their shanty headquarters.

By the late 1970s, 158 Missionaries of Charity "foundations" had been established all over the world. Jim Towey explains that the process of expansion to a new locale typically began because she knew a bishop in the area and received an invitation from him to set up. Then, he says, she followed the spirit. "She read the invitation, prayed over it, and then decided."

After that, the work could start very quickly. Tom Owens, a former IBM executive turned computer entrepreneur who volunteered to help Teresa build an orphanage in Mexico, remembers her sketching out a design for the place on a napkin at one sitting. Except for one detail, the design worked well. At the meeting Teresa asked for a "TB room" to isolate children with tuberculosis. Owens misheard her request as "TV room." He built a state-of-the-art television complex. Later it was repurposed.

Teresa was also capable of waiting. She would open a house in a difficult part of the world only when she felt a suitably resolute and capable nun was available to run it. And she increased the size of her enterprise by organizing auxiliaries. Early on she sought and received Vatican permission to establish a category of volunteers called "co-workers." In the course of a working day the volunteers were often as hands-on in their ministry to the poor as any of the Missionaries. But then they went home, often to comfortable or even palatial residences. Many were also prodigious fundraisers who brought in millions of dollars. Since several of them were globetrotting businessmen or their wives, they proved crucial in advising the order's non-Indian branches.

Many of the co-workers were not Catholic—or even Christian. As Teresa noted during her campaign to have their status recognized officially by the Vatican, for every Christian who had aided her in India, there were 10 non-Christians, and her Roman supervisors accepted that co-workers should be "of all religions and denominations ... who seek to love God in their fellow men." As Teresa biographer Kathryn Spink points out, this may have made the Missionaries the first Catholic religious order to formally affiliate with lay non-Catholics.

Teresa loved to cite concrete results. Spink recalls her ticking off the 1984 totals: 4 million lepers served by mobile clinics since the first of them were sent out in the 1950s; 157,851 people fed at relief centers, 13,246 admitted to homes for the dying and destitute—of whom 8,627 actually ended up living. As she told Spink, "I did not know that our work would grow so fast or go so far."

God did the writing, she liked to say, and she was just the "little pencil." Yet the pencil was endlessly ambitious on behalf of the writer. "If there are poor on the moon," Teresa once declared, "we shall go there too."

And she undoubtedly would have donned a spacesuit herself. By the 1970s Teresa had become a very frequent flier. This was the decade that marked the beginning of what Teresa biographer Eileen Egan called the "flying trapeze" phase of her life, when she was in constant motion, a phase that continued until her death. In 1973, Indira Gandhi gave her a pass for free travel on any Indian Airlines flight. Jim Towey remembers his first day on the job as her lawyer: "The next thing I knew she was giving me her passport and asking me to get her five visas in one day."

Egan traveled with Teresa from May to December 1976, when her itinerary went roughly this way: Bombay (hospice opening); Rome (to accept the gift of a monastery); New York City (visiting a Missionaries of Charity home in the Bronx); Chicago (conference); Omaha (lecture); New York City (mission visit); Tulsa (lecture); Guatemala (earthquake); Mexico City (mission visit); Boston (mission visit); Pennsylvania, Massachusetts, and New York State (three honorary degrees); Vancouver, Canada (conference); Philadelphia (conference); Camden, N.J. (parish visit); Lippstadt, Germany (co-workers' meeting); Taize, France (visit to an ecumenical community); Singapore (conference)—then "home" to Calcutta. Reporters with questions waited at almost every airport. As Egan puts it, "It seemed that Mother Teresa was the practitioner of a special apostolate, the airport sermon."

Even as her mission enlarged, her personality did not appear to change. She attended Mass daily, finding priests to celebrate the Latin version long after the Second Vatican Council freed congregations to hear the liturgy in their own languages. She retained her fondness for small plastic figures of the Virgin Mary. She also retained her sense of urgency and her extremely dry Eastern European humor. (Once, at the end of a conference call with some nuns who had volunteered to stay in a war zone, she told them, "Call me back when you are dead.") At any Missionaries of Charity house she happened to visit, she happily pitched in to do the dirtiest work.

British journalist Malcolm Muggeridge, who was one of the first to bring Teresa to the attention of a large audience, described her this way: "I never experienced so perfect a sense of human equality as with Mother Teresa among the poor." All her life she continued to charm strangers with catchphrases. "Let's do something beautiful for God" was one of them. Another was "You. Did. This. To. Me."—five words that she counted off one by one on the fingers of her listeners, to remind them of Christ's words to his disciples in the Book of Matthew that whenever they helped "one of the least of these my brethren, ye have done it unto me."

By the mid-1970s some of those fingers were on rather powerful hands. As Spink writes, "[She] had a way of involving the right influential people and making them feel they were specially chosen instruments for a divine purpose." The list of what might be called "Executive Branch Co-Workers" came to include President Ronald Reagan, Britain's Prince Charles, India's Prime Minister Indira Gandhi, the Palestinian leader Yasir Arafat, New York City Mayor Ed Koch, and a UN's worth of others. Usually such relationships directly benefited one or another of the Missionaries' projects. But Egan also describes accompanying Teresa to Washington, D.C., in 1974, where, at the invitation of Sen. Hubert H. Humphrey, Teresa spoke affectingly before the Senate Foreign Relations Committee on the subject of U.S. food aid to foreign nations generally.

With ever more influential admirers came ever greater prizes. In 1962, Teresa received the Ramon Magsaysay Award for International Understanding, which is given to leaders who address development problems in Asia in creative ways. Over time she was seen by an ever-widening list of organizations as a perfect inspirational figure for a world in constant need of them, and in the '70s the pace greatly accelerated. In 1971 she was awarded the first Pope John XXIII Peace Prize. Eight months later came the Joseph P. Kennedy Jr. Foundation Prize. In 1973 the first Templeton Prize for progress in religion came her way. Year after year the awards and honors kept arriving.

On Dec. 10, 1979, the tiny stooped nun in her trademark sari and sandals stood in the Grand Hall of Oslo University to accept the greatest honor of them all: the Nobel Prize for Peace. Addressing a room packed with royalty and dignitaries of every nation, she talked, predictably yet movingly, of Christ dying on the cross "for the poor and leprous as well as the healthy and wealthy." But she also moved on to more controversial ground when she told her listeners — in her somewhat broken but perfectly clear English —that "the greatest destroyer of peace today is abortion, because it is a direct war, a direct killing, direct murder by the mother herself." Then she added, "If a mother can kill her own child, what is left—for me to kill you and you to kill me? There is nothing in between."

Teresa's views on abortion did not come as a surprise—she was after all a Catholic nun. But the Nobel acceptance speech made them a focus of attention. And to many who up until that time knew only pastel-colored, broad-brush portraits of Mother Teresa, they complicated the picture. So did her opposition to birth control. It was in the years immediately following the Nobel that the first sustained criticisms of Teresa began to appear, especially in the West. Winning the prize may have been the high point of her recognition as a beloved public figure. But it also inaugurated the period during which Teresa would experience full-on the harshly klieg-lit phenomenon—and very mixed blessing—that is modern fame.

HOME BASE *Women await food at the mission house in Calcutta, still the heart of Teresa's ministry.*

BLESSED EVENT
In Boston, Teresa
blesses an infant
in a neonatal
intensive-care unit.

Global Reach

Teresa seldom attempted to open her mission houses in places she had not been invited. But she encouraged invitations, and over the years she got hundreds, so that by the time of her death the Missionaries of Charity had established facilities in most nations. One that refused to ask her help was China, though several houses still in operation were established in Hong Kong before China absorbed the territory in 1997.

ANTIWAR WARRIOR
In 1982, Teresa drew more than 20,000 people to a peace rally in Toronto.

BELFAST *In 1971, amid strife between Catholics and Protestants, Teresa opened a mission in Northern Ireland.*

NEW YORK CITY *With a police escort during a 1996 visit*

BEIRUT *With children she rescued in Lebanon's civil wa[r]*

PE TOWN *With South Africa's Desmond Tutu in 1988*

WARSAW *Comforting a child during a visit to Poland*

IJING *Outside the Temple of Heaven in 1985*

MADRID *In Spain in 1983 for an anti-abortion Mass*

WASHINGTON, D.C. *Opening a new mission house in 1981*

My Teresa

By SUSAN VAN HOUTE

FIRST PERSON | The first time my father saw me, I was in a shoebox. It was at Mother Teresa's original home for the poor in Calcutta in November 1967, the month I was born. I was so small because I had been born severely undernourished and had chicken pox and the measles. I was basically almost dead. What I was told later was that my birth mother was at Mother Teresa's residence for expectant women, and that she personally went to Teresa and asked her to find a home for me. I don't know what happened to her afterward. Maybe she was able to go home. Maybe she was so sick she just crawled into an alley and died. She just wanted to make sure I had a life, or a chance in life. She had named me Shukulla, which means "love."

REUNITED *Teresa with van Houte and daughter Alyshia in 1995*

In the late 1960s my adoptive father, Dr. John G. Banwell, was a British gastroenterologist teaching in Calcutta and working on a research project on cholera. He and his American-born wife adopted me when I was 3 months old, but it was three months later before the nuns could release me to them because of my illnesses. Later, when I asked why he picked me, he said it was because of my big, big beautiful eyes. Bengali women are known for their big almond-shaped eyes. The nuns who took care of me gave me a simple little pearl on a necklace as a gift when I left the orphanage. Except for the adoption certificate, that's the only actual thing I own from them.

I grew up as a doctor's daughter, which is a comfortable life. I know it's strange, coming from the slums of Calcutta and not knowing what poverty is like. A few years ago I went to see *Slumdog Millionaire*, and I had an anxiety attack. I thought, "That was me! That could have been me!" And I was filled with shame and gratitude and all these things at the same time.

I didn't think much about Mother Teresa when I was growing up. I had my own drama. Adoption is great, but it also creates lots of problems. I had abandonment issues, and there were many family tensions. We moved to the U.S. when I was 2, and I went to private schools from sixth through 12th grade. It was a very privileged life. When I was a teenager, I had an identity crisis. Kids look in the mirror and ask, Gee, do I look like Mom or Dad? But I had no idea. I didn't know whether I had biological siblings.

I had seen Mother Teresa in the news. I knew that she was a Roman Catholic and a remarkable human and someone people should take their hats off to. But it took time for it to sink in—that she was the reason for this amazing fact that I'm alive. I finally wrote to her when I was pregnant with my first daughter, Alyshia Grace. I knew that normal pregnant women usually share everything with their mothers, so in a way I was trying to reconnect with my past. I let her know I was living in Maine with my boyfriend, Hans van Houte, and that we were expecting a baby in April. She wrote me back, saying it was good to hear from me. But she also suggested that Hans and I get married eventually out of the fruitfulness of love.

Well, of course she would say that. I never really thought we needed to be married. We were young, and Hans and I weren't really ready. But getting that letter and being raised Episcopalian—here was a person who really is holier than thou. So eventually it did happen. On Sept. 26, 1992. We now have three beautiful girls: Alyshia Grace, Annika Justine, and Annelies Marie van Houte. A Dutch/Indian mix.

I finally met Mother Teresa in 1995. I had heard on the news that she was coming to New Bedford, Mass., which was 90 minutes from where I was living at the time. Suddenly I had this urge to see her. I gathered the girls in the middle of the night and drove to New Bedford. At dawn I knocked on the door of the Missionaries of Charity house there and explained myself. A few days later the superior nun called to tell me she had set aside tickets for me and my family for the prayer service with Mother Teresa, even though it was booked solid.

Afterward, I was invited into a special prayer session at the Missionaries' house, which was across from the church. It was a very small group. I sat right next to Mother Teresa, and she held my hand for an entire hour. Annika was 6 months old, and she held Annika in her lap while Annika sucked on Teresa's wooden rosary beads.

Holding hands with Mother Teresa told a million stories. The feel of her hands—they were callused and old—and they were the hands that had saved all those lives. Wow, how amazing, for her to be holding me, what an honor and a privilege.

```
+ LDM   July '91                    Calcutta

Dear Susan Shukla,

Thank you for writing to let me know how you are.
Little Alyshia is God's gift of love to you. I pray
that all will go well for you and that you will get
married soon as the fullness and fruitfulness of love
can only be found in marriage which is total and true
giving of yourself to your husband in unconditional
love. I am not sure when I will be in the US next. But
if you keep in touch with our Sisters there, they would
let you know. Sr.M.Dolores MC or Sr.M.Regis MC
Missionaries of Charity, 335 East, 145th St, Bronx,
New York, 10451 Tel/ 212/292 0019. May Mary the Mother
of Jesus be Mother to you and help you bring up your
little one in the love of God and of her own.
```

God bless you
M.c Teresa MC

MOTHER KNOWS BEST *After van Houte wrote to Mother Teresa with the news that she was pregnant but unmarried, Teresa replied with some motherly advice.*

Then Mother Teresa blessed Hans and me and the girls. She touched our heads and chanted her Hail Marys. I had never heard so many Hail Marys in my life as I did in that hour. There was no real conversation—the time was for prayer. I did hug her and give her a kiss, and I was able to whisper in her ear, "Thank you for saving my life." Hans took a picture, and we have it framed on our kitchen wall.

A couple of years later she died. The *Boston Globe* ran Hans's photo and a story, and I ended up on the national news. I tried to stay up and watch the funeral that night and was mad at myself for falling asleep; it was five in the morning. I felt a lot of sorrow, and then I felt so lucky I had had a chance to meet her.

To me she has always been a saint, whether she's canonized yet or not. To me saint is a person that's gone out of her way. Mother Teresa and Lady Diana died so close together, and all anybody could talk about was Diana. Diana was also touched by Mother Teresa, and she had a wonderful heart, and what she did to help clear up the land mines was wonderful. But you can't compare them. Diana was a princess, and then she was a celebrity. Celebrities do something good, and they go back to their rich lifestyles. Mother Teresa totally dedicated her life to doing good, day in and day out. Who else does that? She's the bomb.

I have lived out here on Bainbridge Island in Washington State for the past ten years. It would be a good time now to explain to my daughter Annelies, who is 10, the story of what our family endured. Annelies wasn't born yet when we met Mother Teresa back in Boston. I'll point to the photo on the wall in our kitchen and tell her, "My mommy came to Mother Teresa when she was poor and sick, because she helped save people daily and dedicated her life to it—and I'm the living proof."

You know, 15 years ago when I sat with Mother Teresa in New Bedford, there was another woman at the prayer service. She was living in the Missionaries house; she was like a client. And she was going to have a baby. And that made me think of where I came from. Like, "Here we go again!" Isn't that weird how that worked? I wonder where her baby is now.

Susan van Houte, the mother of three daughters, lives on Bainbridge Island, Washington.

Hello, World

Teresa began to emerge as a global celebrity in 1967, when the BBC broadcast an interview with her conducted by journalist Malcolm Muggeridge (above). Two years later Muggeridge ventured to Calcutta to produce a full-length documentary about Teresa and then a bestselling book. With that she became a constant focus of media attention. At right, photographers swarm as she arrives at the Vatican in 1980.

EYES ON THE PRIZE
On Dec. 10, 1979,
Mother Teresa accepts
the Nobel Peace Prize
in the Grand Hall of
Oslo University.

Superstar

CHAPTER FIVE | In June 1997, Mother Teresa's legal counsel, Jim Towey, felt obligated to update his boss on the latest status of the cinnamon bun case. A Nashville coffee shop owner had announced that one of his pastries bore the likeness of Mother Teresa. Now the man was e-marketing the crusty portrait (the Nun Bun) on T-shirts, coffee mugs, and bookmarks. Towey, looking to rein in the commercialization of Teresa's image, negotiated a settlement allowing the entrepreneur to sell the items locally but not internationally. But when the time came to explain the outcome to Teresa, Towey felt sheepish. By that year she was 87 and wheelchair-bound and had passed leadership of the Missionaries of Charity on to Sister Nirmala, one of

A ROYAL PRESENCE
Princess Diana and Teresa wave to residents of a housing project in the South Bronx during a June 1997 visit to Teresa's Queen of Peace Home in New York City.

her early protégés. Surely she had more important things to think about? Nonetheless, Towey briefed her. With the look of someone who may possibly have had enough, Teresa responded, "Sister Nirmala is now Superior General. Let them put her face on the T-shirt."

That was unlikely. Fame and sainthood are related. For hundreds of years they were almost the same thing, because one of fame's components was heroic virtue, whether on the battlefield, on a throne, or at a pulpit. Yet in the past several centuries the two concepts have diverged dramatically, which is why Zygmunt Szczesny Felinski, a 19th-century archbishop of Warsaw, is a saint (as of October 2009) but not famous, and Mick Jagger is famous but no saint. Very few people—Billy Graham, Pope John Paul II, and the Dalai Lama come to mind—have fulfilled the qualifications for both religious and secular exaltation. For the last 15 years of her career Teresa was one of that select group. She was saintly, and also an icon, a brand, a superstar.

The original catalyst for her worldwide fame was the British writer and television personality Malcolm Muggeridge, a lifelong agnostic turned Christian convert. (Years later, partly at Teresa's urging, he would become a Catholic.) His first interview with Teresa in 1967 was a modest segment for the BBC. But audience reaction was tremendous, so two years later the BBC sent Muggeridge to Calcutta to do a full-length documentary centering on life at the Mother House. His crew captured members of Mother Teresa's order both in contemplation and in charitable action. They followed her through the slums, into her Home for the Dying—which was so dimly lit that Muggeridge later described his success in capturing it on film as "the first authentic photographic miracle"—and to a clinic for lepers, where, on camera, Muggeridge wiped away tears and had to walk out of the frame.

Tears aside, today the documentary seems fairly dry. But Muggeridge's accompanying book, which became an international bestseller, gives some sense of the impression of Teresa it created for millions of viewers at the time. "Something of God's universal love has rubbed off on Mother Teresa," he wrote, "giving her homely features a noticeable luminosity, a shining quality." Even the author Christopher Hitchens, a relentless critic of both Muggeridge and Teresa, acknowledged the impact of Muggeridge's projects. "It is with this film and this book," he wrote, "that we can date the arrival of Mother Teresa's 'image' on the international retina."

India had already put that image on a postage stamp, but now the floodgates of international fame truly opened. In 1975 the New York Times headlined a page-one story about a meeting she attended with the words SPIRITUAL PARLEY HEARS LIVING SAINT. A few months later Time magazine put Teresa on the cover for a pre-Christmas story called LIVING SAINTS: MESSENGERS OF LOVE AND HAPPINESS. Teresa was interviewed by Barbara Walters. The anthropologist Margaret Mead kissed her hand, and Elizabeth Kübler-Ross, godmother to the modern hospice movement, sought her out. Perhaps her greatest admirer was Pope John Paul II. Towey recalls them as the "dynamic duo." As he says, "They had the respect of people of all faiths, and of the irreligious."

At first public recognition seems to have bothered Teresa, who was terrified of committing the sin of pride. She repeatedly joked that her discomfort at being photographed was so great that for every snapshot taken of her a soul should be released from purgatory. But over time she developed a hearty symbiosis with the limelight. Her pithy, earthy style produced natural soundbites. And her image was perfectly camera-ready. She was the opposite of Oscar Wilde's literary creation Dorian Gray. If Gray sold his soul to gain lifelong beauty while his portrait aged, Teresa's creased and weathered face seemed to illustrate her saintliness, mapping every bit of the suffering of others that she had taken on.

HELPING HAND *Hillary Clinton with Teresa at the 1995 dedication of a home in Washington, D.C., for new mothers and their infants*

She learned to exploit those assets. Perhaps the keenest analysis of her in this stage of her mission was offered by the rock star Bob Geldof, the organizer of the first great rock-and-roll charity singalong, "Do They Know It's Christmas?" The two met in the Ethiopian capital of Addis Ababa. "There was nothing otherworldly or divine about her," he later recalled. "The way she spoke to journalists showed her to be as deft a manipulator as any high-powered American public relations expert." Yet, he added, "she was totally selfless. Every moment her aim seemed to be 'How can I use this or that situation to help others?'"

However, while some saints spend their whole lives in seclusion pursuing their particular mode of holiness, superstar saints are tempted, or even obliged, to speak out on a wider range of issues. The better known she became, the more Pope John Paul II and others turned to her to express the Vatican's position on abortion, which she did with her customary energy. "Abortion is nothing but the fear of the child," she said after receiving an honorary doctorate from a university in Rome. "Fear of having to feed one more child, to have to educate one more child, to have to love one more child. Therefore the child must die." At the same time, after receiving the Nobel, she also began more actively to take on the role of peacemaker, as her 1982 visit to wartime Beirut illustrates. Thus, more than any other major church figure, she embodied a holistic concept of "pro-life," beginning at conception, commencing with Christ's love during life, and ending with a dignified death.

Teresa's positions on social issues could place her simultaneously at several different points of the American political spectrum. For instance, in June 1981 she spoke before a high-powered gathering convened by the anti-abortion American Family Institute. Next she had lunch with President Ronald Reagan, reportedly suggesting that the experience of his own near assassination might bring him closer to the suffering of the poor. (Asked later about the conversation, Reagan replied, "I listened.") Finally, in a follow-up note she warned him that "just as abortion is used to kill the unborn child, [nuclear weapons] will become a means to eliminate the Poor of the World—our brothers and sisters whom Jesus has taught us to love."

Over time the world also became more aware of her conservative brand of Catholicism. At the Second Vatican Council in 1962–65, her church expressed its desire to become more open and engage the modern world. Teresa was part of a centuries-old tradition of powerful female "founders" in a male-dominated church, but many of her instincts reflected her extensive pre–Vatican II religious training. Thus, although one effect of the council was that believers could thereafter attend Mass in their own language, she stuck with the traditional Latin version. And her notion of family, which she saw as a weapon to battle poverty, was based on traditional roles of husband and wife. She worried that women in the West, even those with religious vows, were overly ambitious to take on male roles. In a letter to a group of U.S. bishops who were studying the role of nuns, she asked them "to help our religious sisters in the USA to turn to [the Pope] with childlike confidence and love" as a way to counteract "misguided advice and zeal."

Consequently Teresa's fame bred dismay on the part of some liberals inside and outside the church. Feminist Germaine Greer pointed angrily to a statement by Teresa in which she encouraged women who had been raped during the Bangladesh war of independence to bear what Greer called "the offspring of hate" rather than consider abortion. Some American nuns and journalists accused her of promoting female "docility to authority." Others observed that for all her concern for the poor, Teresa never addressed the problem of governments or social systems that ignored or enforced poverty, forgoing the chance to speak in the larger prophetic voice of people like Gandhi and the Reverend Dr. Martin Luther King Jr.

The critique from the left reached its saw-toothed peak in the 1990s with the work of journalist Christopher Hitchens in the documentary *Hell's Angel* and a book called *The Missionary Position*. Unlike some of Teresa's critics, Hitchens was unburdened by any admiration for his subject, whom he described as "a religious fundamentalist, a political operative, a primitive sermonizer, and an accomplice of worldly, secular powers." One of his accusations was that she preferred to share the suffering of the poor and sick than to actually heal them. Hitchens claimed this led to her general preference for building hospices to assist the dying toward death rather than medical centers to treat them, and like other critics he charged that she undermedicated the pain of the perishing and even let curable patients perish for want of significant medical effort. He also wrote that she was willing to befriend despots like the Haitian dictator Baby Doc Duvalier and racketeers like the 1980s-era savings-and-loan criminal Charles Keating as long as they assisted her order.

Teresa answered some of the criticism herself. "We all have a duty to serve God where we feel called," she wrote. "I feel called to help individuals, not to interest myself in structures or institutions. I do not feel like judging or condemning." About Hitchens, she paraphrased Jesus: "May God forgive him; he doesn't know what he is doing." Her champions have been more specific. Regarding the Duvaliers, Towey points out that she also dealt when necessary with Eastern European despots and Fidel Castro. "Was her image exploited?" Towey asks. "I suspect so. But she saw her job as opening houses in their countries and getting supplies in, and she was very focused on that." He also says that once he explained to her what Keating was accused of, Teresa stopped taking Keating's money.

Her supporters say that if the medical care in her houses for the dying was not up to the Western state-of-the-art, it has steadily improved and is frequently better than other local options. She didn't build medical centers, they say, because such centers inevitably cherry-pick those most likely to survive and slough off the worst cases, the people who are "Jesus in his most distressing disguise." Finally—and this is probably hardest for those outside Teresa's mindset to understand—they explain that the austerity, the insistence on personal contact, and the occasional amateurism of the Sisters are expressions of what might be called a philosophy of mutuality. The nuns and their clients were engaged together in a personal transaction to share both Christ's love and his suffering. People like Hitchens point out that the clients might prefer simply to be helped, but are in no position to object. Yet that religious rationale was central to Teresa, who insisted again and again that her missionaries "are not social workers." In fact, they are both something more and something less.

These controversies hardly dented Mother Teresa's general popularity. In both 1981 and 1982 she topped the list compiled by *Good Housekeeping* of the most admired women in the world. While other orders of nuns were suffering a decline in membership, hers continued to grow. Her most trusted sisters became global travelers themselves, supervising new mission houses. Even if the publicity she received was sometimes "all out of proportion to what she actually did," as Spink suggests, Teresa and her co-workers indisputably did a lot. As Spink writes, "Eight hundred thousand capsules of Lampren sent from Switzerland to the lepers in West Bengal;

5,000 tons of high-quality processed food dispatched at a week's notice to the famine-stricken people of Ethiopia and Tanzania—these were some measure of Mother Teresa's impact."

In June 1983, after falling out of bed, Teresa endured a lengthy stay in the hospital. Doctors told her later that were it not for that sustained period of bed rest, she would probably have suffered a heart attack before much longer. For the remaining years of her life, she was in and out of clinics for one or another cardiovascular procedure. But she refused to slow her pace any more than absolutely necessary. "She never said no," Sister Dorothy recalls. "Even to the last."

There would be two great campaigns in her later years. One was to open houses for people suffering from AIDS. The other was to bring the Missionaries of Charity to communist nations. Long before the Berlin Wall came down in 1989, she had founded houses of her order in Poland and East Germany. After the Wall fell, she set up shop almost immediately in Russia, Romania, and Czechoslovakia. But China rebuffed her many efforts. And then there was the very personal issue of Albania. In 1970, on a trip to Macedonia, Teresa visited her hometown of Skopje, but by that time her mother and sister, Aga, had moved to the Albanian capital of Tirana. Albania remained closed to Teresa's ministry until 1991, and by then both women had died. Their last sight of their beloved Gonxha had been at the train station in 1928, when she left home to join the Sisters of Loreto.

Those around her recall that Teresa "mellowed" in her last years, becoming more collaborative in her decision-making and more physically demonstrative in her friendships, accepting hugs from women and even from men. One particular high-profile friendship would be branded in the public mind. Teresa first met Britain's Princess Diana in 1992. Their next encounter, later that year in London, took place as Diana's marital troubles were becoming public. Over five years they met once more in England, and then in the Bronx, N.Y., where photographers captured the image of a smiling Diana towering over her diminutive friend, only months after Teresa's umpteenth hospitalization for her heart problem.

The photo was peculiar and somehow moving. One wondered what they talked about, but you couldn't help but be happy they had found each other, the one so frail and the other so emotionally wounded. Perhaps each was acting on advice that Spink reported Teresa to have given the princess earlier—that when one is in pain, the best thing to do is reach out to others who are suffering, and they will reach out in return.

And then, quite unexpectedly, they died within a week of each other. Diana's fatal car crash occurred on Aug. 31, 1997. On Sept. 5, Teresa's heart finally gave out. As it happens, her last public statement had been about Diana's love for the poor. T-shirts produced almost immediately after Teresa's death imagined her and Diana standing together in heaven wearing matching halos.

In subsequent years some have found it a little odd that the death of one of the world's greatest souls would be nearly overshadowed by the tragedy of her young friend. But of course that was only superficially true. Beyond the fact of the tens of thousands of Calcuttans who crowded to see the body of their adopted "mother" as it was borne to her funeral mass, Teresa had founded an order now numbering over 4,000 sisters in five continents. She had touched millions of lives, and had produced a profound and influential understanding—for her church and for the world—of the sometimes lightly uttered word "charity."

And, oh, yes—she would make news at least twice more. Once with the posthumous publication of a set of astonishing letters that provoked a full-scale worldwide reassessment of her life. And again, less unexpectedly, as her church began the process of making Teresa's saintliness—assumed by millions during her lifetime—official.

BELOVED
In Hyderabad, India, on the 11th anniversary of Teresa's death, a priest leads nuns in prayer before her statue.

The Crowdpleaser

Mother Teresa was so shy she had someone substitute for her at her first public speaking engagement and was shocked in 1960 when photographers met her at a German airport. But by the time she had won a Nobel, done the American talk shows, and publicly befriended notables from Ronald Reagan to Edward Kennedy to Princess Diana, she was as much a folk icon as her champion and ally Pope John Paul II (at right, visiting her in Calcutta in 1986).

GRIN AND GREET
During a 1986 visit to the White House, Teresa and an associate, Sister Frederick, share a laugh with Ronald Reagan.

ADMIRATION SOCIETY

By 1980, the year this picture was taken near Calcutta, Teresa had legions of fans and followers everywhere.

QUEEN ELIZABETH II *In 1983 the Queen presented Teresa with a British honor in New Delhi.*

BOB GELDOF *With the rocker humanitarian in 1985*

PRINCE CHARLES *With Teresa in Calcutta in 1980*

POPE JOHN PAUL II *Mother Teresa shares a word with the Holy Father at Saint Peter's Cathedral in Rome in 1997.*

YASIR ARAFAT *With the Palestinian leader in 1990*

SEN. EDWARD KENNEDY *In Calcutta in 1971*

THE DALAI LAMA *They met in England in 1988.*

Her Agony

CHAPTER SIX

In August 2007, eight years after
Teresa's death, a new book appeared called *Mother
Teresa: Come Be My Light.* So gentle was the title that
a casual bookstore browser might have mistaken it for
one more pious rehash of her career. That would have been a huge
misjudgment. The book was biographical dynamite.

In format it was simple enough: a collection of Teresa's letters
written over five decades that had been gathered by Father Brian
Kolodiejchuk, a member of the branch of Teresa's order established
for priests. He was also the man who had been chosen soon after
her death to be her "postulator." That's the person tapped by the
Catholic Church to research the life of anyone being considered for

mind my feelings– Don't mind even– my pain If my separation from You– brings others to You and in their love and company– You find joy and pleasure. Why Jesus, I am willing with all my heart to suffer all that I suffer– not only now– but for all eternity – if this was possible. Your happiness is all that I want– for the rest– please do not take the trouble– even if You see me faint with pain.– All this is my Will– I want to satiate Your Thirst with every single drop of blood that You can find in me.– Don't allow me to do You wrong in any way. Take from me the power of hurting You.– Heart and soul I will work for the Sisters– because they are Yours. Each and every one– are Yours. I beg of You only one thing– please do not take the trouble to return soon.– I am ready to wait for You for all eternity.–

Your little one.

ARE YOU THERE? *In 1959, at the suggestion of her then-confessor, Father Lawrence Trevor Picachy, Teresa wrote a letter to Christ describing her anguish and her devotion to Him.*

sainthood and, if appropriate, to make the argument in favor of canonization. (The same Father Kolodiejchuk wrote the next chapter of this book, discussing his experiences in that role.) Kolodiejchuk has argued powerfully that the letters help prove Teresa's holiness. But taken together, they also formed a brutally candid, often excruciatingly sad record of the tormented inner life of a woman ordinarily known for her unflagging cheer. With its more than 150 letters and notes, most of them private communications from Teresa to her formal or informal spiritual advisers, *Come Be My Light* was a biographical game-changer. Its most astonishing revelation was that almost from the moment she began ministering personally to the poorest in 1948 until her death 49 years later, with the exception of a five-week break in 1958, Teresa was utterly unable to feel the presence of God in her life. As Kolodiejchuk put it: "Neither in her heart or in the Eucharist."

In the weeks and months after the book was published, the discussion it aroused was dominated by questions raised by that startling disclosure. Could Mother Teresa have lost her faith? And so early in life? If she had, could she still be a candidate for sainthood? And if it was true that God had withdrawn from her, how could He treat one of His most avid servants this way? *Time* magazine's cover story was headlined simply HER AGONY.

None of those questions were surprising in connection with a book that brought to the world the news that Teresa had suffered a "dark night of the soul" that almost no one knew about. But *Come Be My Light* also added richly to her story in other ways. For one thing the letters—the first of them written in Croatian when Teresa was still in high school, the later ones shifting into her informal, telegraphic English, full of phrases separated by dashes—illustrated the nearly shocking intensity of her spiritual life, her desire to "burn myself completely for Him and souls" and "to be His victim in every way." The book also provided the first blow-by-blow description of her campaign from October 1946 until January 1948 to overcome the initial skepticism of her diocese and her church about her proposed ministry to the very poor. In dozens of letters to her spiritual director, Father Celeste Van Exem, and to Ferdinand Perier, the Archbishop of Calcutta, she employs the weapons of Bible-based appeal, personal plea, partial accommodation, and flat-out demand. "Let me go," she implores Perier. "Souls are being lost in the meantime." At times she even resorts to divine name-dropping, as when she informs Van Exem: "How often, how very often, He complained of delays."

It was as part of this struggle to convince Perier that Teresa produced a written account of the vivid conversations with Jesus and visions of Him that she first experienced on the train to Darjeeling in 1946. (In a supporting note Van Exem wrote to Perier that her "union with Our Lord has been continual and so deep and violent that rapture does not seem very far.") During her lifetime Teresa had described the experience to most of her followers only in the vaguest terms. So for most people the publication of that detailed description in *Come Be My Light* unveiled for the first time the vivid mystical basis of her work.

Above all the book provided a window into the soul of a holy woman whose cataract of spiritual experience appeared to have dried up almost completely after the 40th year of her 87-year life, starting at almost exactly the moment when she initiated her great earthly project.

TWO MONTHS AFTER SHE FOUNDED THE MISSIONARIES OF CHARITY, TERESA WROTE TO PERIER: "What tortures of loneliness. I wonder how long will my heart suffer this?" The precise nature of her loneliness, ill defined at that point, was made more explicit in a letter to her archbishop three years later. "Please pray ... that Our Lord may show Himself—for there is such a terrible

IN THE DARKNESS *Teresa suffered her profound estrangement from God during the very years of her greatest achievement for others.*

darkness within me, as if everything was dead. It has been like this more or less from the time I started 'the work.'"

The letters testify that the "darkness" continued miserably for most of the rest of her life. In 1957 she describes her suffering this way: "Such deep longing for God—and ... repulsed— empty—no faith—no love—no zeal ... Heaven means nothing." Twenty-two years later, in the year she accepted her Nobel Prize, she wrote to a friend, "Jesus has a very special love for you. [But] as for me, the silence and the emptiness is so great, that I look and do not see—listen and do not hear—the tongue moves [in prayer] but does not speak." In more than 40 of the letters and other communications in *Come Be My Light* she laments the "dryness," "darkness," "loneliness," and "torture" she is experiencing because of the disappearance of any feeling of a connection with Jesus.

Confessors, whether formal ones like Archbishop Perier or informal confidants, were a constant in Teresa's spiritual life. As the Missionaries of Charity flourished and won international renown, she accumulated them the way some people do psychotherapists. It was to Perier that she joyfully relayed news of the brief respite in her spiritual despair that she experienced in 1958 after praying to the newly deceased Pope Pius XII. But just five weeks later she reported being "in the tunnel" again. Reading letter after letter, one can draw no other conclusion than that the woman who said "Loneliness and the feeling of being unwanted is the most terrible kind of poverty" spent much of her life in near desolation.

In the mid-1960s Mother Teresa arrived at a kind of resigned solace through communications with Joseph Neuner, a renowned Austrian-born theologian-priest whom she first met after he wrote an article about her for a Catholic magazine in Germany. In letters and in person Neuner told her several things she needed to hear. One was that there was no human remedy for her condition, so she should not feel responsible to affect it. Another was that feeling the presence of Jesus is not the only proof of His being there, that her very craving for God was a "sure sign" of his "hidden presence" in her life, and that his apparent absence could in fact be part of the "spiritual side" of her work for Jesus. These exchanges seemed to lift a great weight from Teresa. In particular she embraced his notion that her spiritual dryness was actually another way for her to share in the Passion of the same Christ who said from the cross, "My God, my God, why have you forsaken me?" Indeed, she took the logic a step further. "I have come to love the darkness," she wrote to Neuner. And later she speculated this way: "If I ever become a saint—I will surely be one of 'darkness.' I will continually be absent from heaven—to [light] the light of those in darkness on earth."

For weeks after the Kolodiejchuk book was published, television anchors and newspaper op-ed writers wrestled with the question of whether Teresa's long spiritual dryness could disqualify her for sainthood. The journalist Christopher Hitchens, her self-appointed nemesis, described her in print as a "confused old lady who had for all practical purposes ceased to believe." Pointing to passages in her letters such as one in which she addressed Jesus directly ("What do I labor for? If there be no God—there can be no soul—if there is no soul, then, Jesus—You also are not true"), Hitchens diagnosed her distress as late-breaking atheism. It was, he said, "the inevitable result of a dogma that asks people to believe impossible things and then makes them feel ... guilty when their innate reason rebels." Hitchens further hypothesized that the things Teresa's critics disliked about her, including her "international crusade against divorce, abortion, and contraception," were symptoms of a "strenuous and almost hysterical effort to drown out the awful fear of 'absence.'"

That seems overdrawn. Only three of Teresa's published letters indicate any doubt about God's existence, while many more attest that, despite all, her will was "steadfast bound" to Christ. But whatever you may think of Hitchens's attempts to psychoanalyze Teresa, it's true that *Come Be My Light* is in some ways the perfect saint's life for a Freudian age. Here is someone we thought was possessed of a cheery, simple piety, but who turned out to have had a complex, even turbulent internal life and to have labored for decades in painful confusion about Christ's intentions for her.

Yet even if some of Teresa's actions sprang from psychological needs, would that make her any less holy? Does her agony make her any less saintly? Certainly her church does not think so. It's worth remembering that Kolodiejchuk presented her letters to the Vatican as part of the argument in favor of her sainthood. After his book was published, many commentators correctly noted that Roman Catholicism long ago identified dark nights of the soul as a stage in the spiritual development of many saints, often a period of purification clearing the way for them to enjoy an even more intimate union with God. But Kolodiejchuk puts forward a more radical reading of her experience, one also advanced by Neuner: that her "abandonment" was more likely to represent an even more profound union with the bleakest moment of Jesus' life, His execution on the cross. Like some other students of Teresa's life, Kolodiejchuk also thinks that her fears of abandonment by Christ may have strengthened her solidarity with those whom the world had discarded. As he puts it, "Mother often said that the greatest poverty in the world, among the affluent, as well as the poorest of the poor, is to be 'unloved, unwanted, and uncared for.' Unbeknownst to almost everyone, she was living this very experience herself, in solidarity, through Christ, with the poorest of the poor. From that perspective, her darkness was not so much a purifying darkness as an apostolic one." (By "apostolic" he means something that helped her in her mission to transmit God's love.) Meanwhile, other observers, notably the Jesuit author Father James Martin, believe that the revelations in *Come Be My Light* have actually created a new, posthumous ministry for Teresa, a ministry to people who have suffered their own episodes of spiritual dryness.

Mother Teresa did not minister in easy times—neither in the chaos of Calcutta in the 1950s nor amid the strange looming tensions of the Cold War. It was an era when nations knew they possessed weapons that could kill millions at one blow. Projecting love the same way was impossible. But Teresa proved that love, individualized love, still made sense in an atomic age, was still effective and meaningful, still redeeming. Thousands followed her and continue to do so; tens of thousands have visited her homes and returned changed and spiritually activated. And millions more allowed themselves to be touched by recognizing the flame of faith and love she represented and to discover at least the flicker of the same within themselves.

We live now in a time when economic globalization has created an awareness of inter-dependence among people and the Internet provides an illusion of intimacy. But the poorest of the poor still remain a people apart, demanding that we identify and act upon the image of the divine in each of them. That commitment remains as pressing—and as essential to the progress of our own souls—as ever. On Aug. 26, 2010, the 100th anniversary of Teresa's birth, the U.S. government issued a postage stamp with her image on it. That's the kind of gesture that usually signals that a person has been relegated safely to history. But some individuals are never just historical, because the message they bear is forever essential. Teresa is one of those. Whatever she is up to now, the "little bud" flowered mightily among us and left us with a vision that should challenge us forever—or until, somehow, we achieve the ideal that she lived.

The Funeral

As she lay in state at Calcutta's Saint Thomas Church, mourners like the boy above paid their respects to Mother Teresa. On Sept. 13, 1997, her body was borne through the streets on a gun carriage that had once carried the body of Gandhi. After the state service she was buried beneath a plain stone at the Mother House on what is now AJC Bose Road. At right, nuns of her order pray at her grave in 2002.

The Cause

By FATHER BRIAN KOLODIEJCHUK, MC

What is a saint? In the Catholic faith a saint is a role model for others and an intercessor in heaven before God. Almost immediately after Mother Teresa's death, many voices were raised in the hope that she would be declared one of these. Within weeks the then archbishop of Calcutta, Henry D'Souza, sought permission from the Congregation for the Causes of Saints in the Vatican to proceed with something the church terms a "cause." This is the process whereby the church determines whether a candidate for sainthood is worthy of that special status. In those first months after her death I had little inkling that the cause of Mother Teresa was one in which I would be deeply involved.

LAST JOURNEY *On Sept. 13, 1997, an Indian military honor guard bears Teresa's coffin to the Mother House for burial.*

REMEMBRANCES *The Catholic faith holds that relics, earthly objects or substances closely associated with a holy person in life, are worthy of veneration after death. The relics seen here are kept at the Missionaries of Charity's Queen of Peace Home in the Bronx, N.Y. Above is a table setting Teresa often used while visiting the house. To the right is a drop of her blood on a gauze pad set within a silver charm.*

Contrary to the popular idea that the Pope "makes" saints, the process is bottom-up, not top-down. The church initiates a cause in response to a preexisting sense on the part of believers—a sense considered to be the work of the Holy Spirit—that someone who recently died exhibited "heroic virtue" while alive. Without waiting for validation from Rome, these believers begin praying for that person to intercede before God on behalf of themselves or their loved ones. If they find that their prayers have been answered and spread the word, that person develops a reputation for sanctity. Only when such a reputation becomes widespread does the church investigate. And in most cases it will not begin that inquiry until at least five years after the death of the candidate for sainthood.

In most cases. In December 1998, little more than a year after Teresa's death, the Congregation for Causes, acting with the approval of Pope John Paul II, waived the five-year rule for her. After all, it was plain that within her lifetime she had already enjoyed a worldwide reputation for holiness. Very soon after her death many thousands of Catholics everywhere were praying for her intercession before God.

That fast-track exemption allowed Teresa's cause to proceed to the next step, the appointment of her "postulator" by the Missionaries of Charity. The postulator is the soul of a cause. He or she must assemble the truth about the candidate, concentrating on the information that indicates sainthood. Out of this raw data the postulator then crafts a report called a *positio*. The purpose of that report is to show how the person in question lived what are called the theological virtues of faith, hope, and charity, as well as the human, moral virtues of prudence, justice, courage (or fortitude), and self-control. The *positio* may go on to focus on topics such as humility, the fulfillment of vows in such matters as chastity, poverty, and obedience, and the candidate's special gifts. The completed report goes to two commissions, one composed of nine theologians and the other of cardinals and bishops. After considering the evidence, the commissions make their recommendations to the Pope.

In March 1999, I was chosen to be Mother Teresa's postulator. I had known her for 20 years—I'm a member of the branch of her order that was established in 1984 for priests. At the time of my appointment, I was aware that many people were expecting a quick process. It seemed to them that this cause should be a slam dunk. Yet I also knew that I had God, the church, and history looking over my shoulder, and so I was determined to fulfill this serious responsibility as best I could, counting on the assistance of key helpers. I did not want simply to go through the motions. If I did an inadequate job, I would be remembered as the one who messed up Mother Teresa's cause. If I did it right, I would be just a footnote, but a happy footnote.

A cause is an extraordinarily thorough process. Once it is initiated, I do not believe that any other institution—not the media, governments, or other religious groups—combs through the life of someone as thoroughly as does the Catholic Church. Beyond its formal role in beatification, which is the step just prior to sainthood, and then in canonization, which is the final stage, a cause is often our best chance to acquire as much information as possible about a holy person from those who knew him or her. There are times when the information is sparse, and you really have to hunt. The situation with Mother Teresa was just the opposite. There were many leads to follow, all around the world. People carrying out the work of the cause sought answers to 263 questions pertaining to her life and her exercise of Christian virtue. After two years of diligent effort, we presented the Congregation for the Causes of Saints with testimony and documents that filled 83 volumes—35,000 pages! Those volumes contained everything from her baptismal certificate to documents on the history of her congregation and letters from

WONDER WOMAN
The 1998 cure of a tumor suffered by Monica Besra (left) was the first miracle credited officially to Teresa.

Mother Teresa seeking guidance from her spiritual directors. Also included was testimony from all kinds of people who knew Mother Teresa or had fresh thoughts about her—among them people who made clear that they were not her admirers.

None of the information was unwanted. Everyone who knew Mother Teresa had his or her own piece of the pie, so to speak, and we were interested in the whole pie. But as the investigation progressed, we realized that, in particular, the testimony of a handful of priests, as well as Mother Teresa's own letters, was unlocking a whole different order of understanding about her, especially regarding hidden aspects of her holiness.

Gradually we became aware of three aspects that have now become part of her public story. One was her almost fierce intent to love Jesus as He had never been loved before. Another concerned the voices she heard and visions she experienced that informed her call to serve the poorest of the poor. Those happened amid an experience of God's closeness to her that was described by one of her early confessors as "continual … deep and violent." Finally, and most surprisingly, there was the decades-long period of distress and loneliness that she endured following the foundation of the Missionaries of Charity, a period that she described as her "darkness."

These were not aspects of herself that Mother Teresa wanted to make public. She recognized that she had received extraordinary gifts but hid them for fear of attracting undue attention to herself. And she was quite successful in this. The world recognized her holiness, but in a fairly superficial sort of way, as a natural complement to her good works, outward cheerfulness, and plainspoken practicality. She was very human—someone who, for example, loved ice cream and a good joke and could be impatient at times. (She went to confession at least once a week for something!) So many people had their lives changed through their contact with her, but only the tiniest fraction of them realized the richness and profundity of her interior life. In fact, the aggregation of the new material reveals her to be a mystic, probably one of the greatest of modern times, if not of the Church's entire history. It compelled us to look at her previous public utterances in a new light. We discovered that they, too, exemplified a profound wisdom and what can truly be characterized as a heroic love for God and neighbor.

To protect the living or the recently deceased, some of this material cannot yet be made public. As its release becomes feasible, the Mother Teresa Center (motherteresa.org) hopes to make it available. But with the support of the Vatican, I was allowed to disseminate some of it in the book *Mother Teresa: Come Be My Light*. I intend to include more in a full-scale biography.

The most striking example of her spiritual heroism was the intimate bond she maintained with Jesus, despite what she termed the long darkness, a period during which He seemed to have retreated from any connection with her that she could discern through prayer. Not even those sisters closest to her had any knowledge of this trial, which was so at odds with the joy and balance she radiated throughout her life. Various saints have experienced "dark nights of the soul." Saint John of the Cross wrote eloquently about it. In their cases the absence of a felt connection to Jesus was believed to have purified the seeker, disposing him or her to a more intimate union with God. But Mother Teresa's trial was different. She achieved her "deep and violent" union at age 36, but then lived for nearly 50 years in an agonizing darkness. While convinced that her fundamental connection to Jesus was "unbroken," at the level of consciousness her soul was like a wasteland.

To me and to the theologians who later examined her case, what was truly remarkable in this was that she was so united to Jesus in pure faith and love that He could share with her some of the intense interior suffering He had experienced in the Garden of Olives and on the cross.

Indeed, this very different kind of union is given to almost no one. Throughout the history of the Church, only a handful of saints lived such an experience for a comparable length of time. Hers was an extraordinary and exceptional call.

BY APRIL 2002, I HAD BOILED DOWN THE 83 VOLUMES OF TESTIMONY AND DOCUMENTS TO A *positio* of about 5,000 pages. On Dec. 21 of that year the Pope, having heard from the commissions that had received the *positio*, decreed Mother Teresa's heroic virtue. From that date she was known as the Venerable Servant of God, Mother Teresa of Kolkata. (This reflected the spelling of Calcutta that the city had adopted in the previous year.) After this declaration, the further progress of a cause depends on miracles. More specifically it depends on the confirmation of miracles, usually medical, that have occurred through the candidate's intercession with God. In this context they serve as God's validation. If there is some unknown reason that should disqualify someone from sainthood, God would not answer a plea addressed to Him through that person.

The Vatican has an involved and rigorous process for vetting miracles, one in which the postulator is again a kind of middleman between local believers and Rome. In this, too, I acted as a conduit. In June 1999 we received in Calcutta a report from the Sisters' community in West Bengal. In September of the previous year a woman named Monica Besra, who had a large and very visible tumor, had stayed with them. After she and the Sisters had prayed for Mother's intercession, the growth, of six to seven inches in length, had disappeared within several hours. On reading the report we thought it could be a strong contender for the necessary first miracle. We gathered medical documentation—from 11 doctors in Calcutta alone—and testimonies, studied them, and submitted them for consideration by the Vatican's Congregation for the Causes of Saints. The doctors, theologians, and bishops who consult for the Congregation unanimously believed that there was no medical explanation for the sudden cure and that therefore Mother Teresa's intercession was responsible. On Dec. 21, 2002, the cure was judged to be a miracle. That paved the way for Mother Teresa's beatification the next year on Oct. 19.

Beatification allows candidates for sainthood to be venerated in their local churches, within their own religious congregations, and in other places by those who receive permission. It's an extraordinary milestone, but still one step away from canonization, which requires a second miracle. As of now we continue to await one, and people continue to report instances, as well as precious testimonies regarding Mother Teresa's life. The "pie" is not yet complete.

God has His own plans and times. But we currently have more than 3,500 reports from every part of the world of supernatural favors attributed to Mother Teresa's intercession. Their range speaks to far more than the typical modern measures for canonization, cases involving cancer or comas. People report healings from drug addiction, marriages reconciled, family rifts mended—everything from school exams passed to peaceful deaths. Those reports reflect the way people understand her and reach out to her. I am certain that when the time is right, a verifiable miracle will be ascertained and the Church will have one more saint among its ranks, Saint Teresa of Kolkata.

Father Brian, who has been the postulator of the Cause of Beatification and Canonization of Mother Teresa since 1999, is also Superior General of the Missionaries of Charity Fathers.

NEARLY SAINTED
On Oct. 19, 2003, more than a quarter-million people flooded Saint Peter's Square in Rome for an open-air Mass to mark Teresa's beatification.

About the Cover

BY MICHAEL COLLOPY

YEARS AGO MOTHER TERESA ASKED ME TO TAKE A FORMAL portrait of her. She did this at the urging of the sisters in the Missionaries of Charity, who wanted an updated picture of her to keep in their prayer books. Though she had agreed to sit for the portrait, she did it somewhat reluctantly. She did not pose comfortably for pictures. She told me that she had a deal with God that for each photo taken of her, a soul was released from purgatory. You can imagine the pressure that put me under.

In fact, one day Mother saw me among a sea of photographers taking pictures of her and came over to me with a big smile, shaking her finger and saying that today "the place" was cleaned out! Only she and I knew what place she meant.

I took the cover portrait on a very warm day in 1987. I set up my lights and a screen in the greeting room adjacent to a chapel at the Missionaries of Charity mission house in San Francisco. Mother came into the room with Sister Frederick, the permanent secretary of the Missionaries of Charity in Calcutta and her frequent traveling companion in those years. I had set my Hasselblad camera on a tripod with a long cable release so that I would not be behind the camera but face to face with Mother. That way, instead of having Mother look into the camera, we could have a conversation as I took pictures, which I hoped would make her more comfortable. As soon as Mother sat down on the stool I had set up, Sister Frederick insisted that she take off her sweater. Then she began to primp Mother's head garment and pin so that she looked right—and they both started to giggle like schoolgirls. Which is what prompted the smile.

Photo Credits